FR DAMIEN &
WHERE ALL ROADS LEAD

Comprising

FR DAMIEN

Robert Louis Stevenson

1956

WHERE ALL ROADS LEAD

G K Chesterton

1961

CATHOLIC TRUTH SOCIETY

PUBLISHERS TO THE HOLY SEE

The man who tried to do what
Damien did, is my father, and the
father of all who love goodness;
and he was your father too, if God
had given you grace to see it.

Robert Louis Stevenson is best known as the author of
Treasure Island. G K Chesterton's prolific writings on
Catholicism are still widely read.

CTS ONEFIFTIES
Father Damien, originally published CTS 1956; reprints an open letter
of 1890. *Where All Roads Lead*, published CTS 1961, reprinting extracts
of material published in *Blackfriars*, 1922-1923.
Published by The Incorporated Catholic Truth Society,
40-46 Harleyford Road, London SE11 5AY
www.ctsbooks.org
ISBN 978 1 78469 527 9

FR DAMIEN

Robert Louis Stevenson

INTRODUCTION

It was like Robert Louis Stevenson, the rebel from the strictness of a lowland manse, the keen searcher and portrayer of the heroic element in human character which tautens weakness and ennobles failure, the invalid who experienced the instinctive repulsion of disease, to write so passionately in vindication of Damien de Veuster. Say if you like that Stevenson was a romantic, that he was inflamed by the gesture made by Fr Damien when, at the consecration of the new church at Waikulu, the Vicar Apostolic of Hawaii asked for volunteers from among his clergy to minister to the needs of the lepers segregated on the island of Molokai, he stepped forward and in doing so made himself a voluntary exile from the cheerful ways of men, an outcast of the people. That this gesture was no sudden enthusiasm, that the sacrifice was persisted in to the end, that never by word or sign did Damien ever show hesitation in his choice or regret for such a resolution it needs no romanticism but only the insight common to generous minds to wonder at and thank God for.

Fr Damien's story is too well known to do more here

than indicate a passing word, an action characteristic of the man, which can give an insight into his personality. He determined from the beginning never to show disgust or repulsion at the decaying bodies, the open sores, the hands from which the fingers had dropped, at any of the loathsome disfigurements of the disease which reduces the human body to a formless mass of corrupting flesh, and his determination carried out was the strength of his apostolate. Hardly had he arrived on Molokai when he was called to give the Last Sacraments to a dying leper, tended in a filthy hut by his mother who was not a Catholic. Damien might have contented himself under the circumstances with one anointing only, he might have availed himself of the dispensation allowed by the Church to anoint with an instrument so that the priest may avoid touching the body of a person suffering from a contagious disease, but he would not do so. With his bare thumb he anointed the sore-infested ears, the eyelids swollen with pus, the gaping hole which was once a mouth, the feet which he discovered were already being gnawed away by worms. The details are nauseating, but without them there is no measure of the self-mastery, the cooperation with grace which lent the priestly office a Christ-like tenderness. It was this surely that caused the mother of the dying man, herself a leper, to beg of Damien as he was about to leave the hut that he would receive her into the Church. When Stevenson visited Molokai a year after Damien's death he wrote over his autograph in the hospital which Damien had built, and to which he had called the Franciscan Sisters to minister, a verse of which one line runs: *Lo, beauty springing from the breast of pain.* This was the vision which the woman saw at the squalid death-bed, and it was the mission of Damien de Veuster to make all the world see it.

The story of the sermon on that Sunday in June twelve years after the beginning of his mission is a famous one, but Damien's secret is that from the start he thought in terms of that simple phrase which has ever since troubled the minds of those who enjoy health and worldly prosperity, "we lepers." It is without question heroic to minister to the needs of lepers, to associate oneself with tenderness with their sufferings and raise them from the degradation of mind and spirit of which such sufferings are the cause. Such a heroism might well look for the occasional hour of recreation apart from the sights and sounds of horror and no one would cast a stone. But not so Damien; perhaps to enter into the pitiable joys of men and women so afflicted is harder even than to tend their sufferings, to administer the Sacraments. In the evenings Damien would sit in his hut, eating his supper surrounded by those lepers who still had the strength to walk there, or even only to crawl there, listening to their stories and reminiscences, telling them in return of his boyhood on the family farm in Belgium, joining in their laughter and their jokes. After supper there would be tea and biscuits all round and Damien would smoke his pipe, offering it to his immediate neighbour who would pass it round after a puff or two. A spectator who came on such a scene unawares might be forgiven for thinking himself an assistant at a feast of ghouls, a Christian must see in it only the reflection of Him who did not shrink from taking human nature and making it His own, bearing our infirmities and carrying our sorrows.

What motives impelled the Rev. Dr Hyde, the Presbyterian Minister at Honolulu, to denigrate the memory of such a man as this? Perhaps, as Stevenson suggests, it was envy, the sense of frustration of the man who sat in his fine house angry at his own failure, jealous of the fame of Damien. I cannot help feeling that Damien, who hated publicity of any kind and once angrily rebuked his own brother for publishing one of his letters from Molokai in a Belgian newspaper, would have felt gratitude to Dr Hyde. "Coarse and dirty" Hyde had called him; to many of their contemporaries, and to many moderns as well, St Francis of Assisi, St Catherine of Siena, St Benedict Joseph Labre have seemed coarse and dirty. That Damien made himself one of the lepers, bringing himself "down to their level," that his contraction of the disease was the result of his mixing with them, "of his own vices and carelessness" was the burden of Dr Hyde's complaint. We have the witness of Joseph Dutton, who, after a remarkable career in the world, came to Molokai as his helper, that there was never question of Damien's purity, and for the rest a man may be pardoned for hearing in Dr Hyde's complaint the tones of another criticism made long ago, "this man eateth and drinketh with publicans and sinners." It is the tragedy of the narrow heart to be unable to see love in the actions of another, to be unable to hear love in the tones of the voice and to attribute the works of pure charity to unworthy motives. We can but wish that Damien's prayers may have won for his critic one glimpse of human and divine charity, one upsurge of generosity before the end.

The significance of the life and sacrifice of Damien de Veuster for an age which looks upon physical fitness and economic progress as ultimate values and a painful death as the greatest evil which can befall a man is this, that they proclaim unmistakably and inescapably the higher value of the human soul. No age could refuse its homage to him whether its values were false ones or true, but that homage of itself compels the admission that whatever may happen to the bodies of men and women as far as this life is concerned their souls are by nature immortal and possess a destiny of happiness which can be achieved by the grace of God or lost for the lack of it. Were it not so, the mission of Damien was the most futile of lost causes, achieving nothing because there was nothing to achieve. That his sacrifice does not make sense is a conclusion very few would be rash enough to draw and still less to maintain. Dr Hyde saw no sacrifice at all, but only the results of vice and carelessness and the world at large has judged him blind, preferring to approve Stevenson's judgment that "the man who tried to do what Damien did is my father…the father of all who love goodness."

G. A. Tomlinson

FATHER DAMIEN

AN OPEN LETTER TO THE REVEREND DR HYDE OF
HONOLULU

Sydney, February 25, 1890.

Sir,—It may probably occur to you that we have met, and visited, and conversed; on my side, with interest. You may remember that you have done me several courtesies, for which I was prepared to be grateful. *But there are duties which come before gratitude,* and offences which justly divide friends, far more acquaintances. Your letter to the Reverend H. B. Gage is a document which, in my sight, if you had filled me with bread when I was starving, if you had sat up to nurse my father when he lay a-dying, would yet absolve me from the bonds of gratitude. You know enough, doubtless, of the process of canonisation to be aware that, a hundred years after the death of Damien, there will appear a man charged with the painful office of the *devil's advocate.* After that noble brother of mine, and of all frail clay, shall have lain a century at rest, one shall accuse, one defend him. The circumstance is unusual that the devil's advocate should be a volunteer, should be a member of a sect immediately rival, and should make haste to take upon himself his ugly office ere the bones are cold; unusual, and of a taste which I shall leave my readers free to qualify; unusual, and to me inspiring. If I have at all learned the trade of using words to convey truth and to arouse emotion, you have at last furnished me with a subject. For it is in the interest of all mankind, and the cause of public decency in every quarter of the world, not only that Damien should be righted, but that you and your letter should be displayed at length, in their true colours, to the public eye.

To do this properly, I must begin by quoting you at large: I shall then proceed to criticise your utterance from several points of view, divine and human, in the course of which I shall attempt to draw again, and with more specification, the character of the dead saint whom it has pleased you to vilify: so much being done, I shall say farewell to you for ever.

"Honolulu, August 2, 1889.

"Rev. H. B. Gage.

"Dear Brother,—In answer to your inquiries about Father Damien, I can only reply that we who knew the man are surprised at the extravagant newspaper laudations, as if he was a most saintly philanthropist. The simple truth is, he was a coarse, dirty man, headstrong and bigoted. He was not sent to Molokai, but went there without orders; did not stay at the leper settlement (before he became one himself), but circulated freely over the whole island (less than half the island is devoted to the lepers), and he came often to Honolulu. He had no hand in the reforms and improvements inaugurated, which were the work of our Board of Health, as occasion required and means were provided. He was not a pure man in his relations with women, and the leprosy of which he died should be attributed to his vices and carelessness. Others have done much for the lepers, our own ministers, the government physicians, and so forth, but never with the Catholic idea of meriting eternal life.—

Yours, etc.,

C. M. HYDE."[1]

To deal fitly with a letter so extraordinary, I must draw at the outset on my private knowledge of the signatory and his sect. It may offend others; scarcely you, who have been so busy to collect, so bold to publish, gossip on your rivals. And this is perhaps the moment when I may best explain to you the character of what you are to read: I conceive you as a man quite beyond and below the reticences of civility: with what

From the Sydney *Presbyterian*, October 26, 1889.

measure you mete, with that shall it be measured you again; with you, at last, I rejoice to feel the button off the foil and to plunge home. And if in aught that I shall say I should offend others, your colleagues, whom I respect and remember with affection, I can but offer them my regret; I am not free, I am inspired by the consideration of interests far more large; and such pain as can be inflicted by anything from me must be indeed trifling when compared with the pain with which they read your letter. It is not the hangman, but the criminal, that brings dishonour on the house.

You belong, sir, to a sect—I believe my sect, and that in which my ancestors laboured—which has enjoyed, and partly failed to utilise, an exceptional advantage in the islands of Hawaii. The first missionaries came; they found the land already self-purged of its old and bloody faith; they were embraced, almost on their arrival, with enthusiasm; what troubles they supported came far more from whites than from Hawaiians; and to these last they stood (in a rough figure) in the shoes of God. This is not the place to enter into the degree or causes of their failure, such as it is. One element alone is pertinent, and must here be plainly dealt with. In the course of their evangelical calling, they—or too many of them—grew rich. It may be news to you that the houses of missionaries are a cause of mocking on the streets of Honolulu. It will at least be news to you, that when I returned your civil visit, the driver of my cab commented on the size, the taste, and the comfort of your home. It would have been news certainly to myself, had any one told me that afternoon that I should live to drag such matter into print. But you see, sir, how you degrade better men to your own level; and it is needful that those who are to judge betwixt you and me, betwixt Damien and the devil's advocate, should understand your letter to have been penned in a house which could raise, and that very justly, the envy and the comments of the passers-by. I think (to employ a phrase of yours which I admire) it "should be attributed" to you that you have never visited the scene of Damien's life and death. If you had, and had recalled it, and looked about your pleasant rooms, even your pen perhaps would have been stayed.

Your sect (and remember, as far as any sect avows me, it is mine) has not done ill in a worldly sense in the Hawaiian Kingdom. When calamity befell their innocent parishioners, when leprosy descended and took root in the Eight Islands, a *quid pro quo* was to be looked for. To that prosperous mission, and to you, as one of its adornments, God had sent at last an opportunity. I know I am touching here upon a nerve acutely sensitive. I know that others of your colleagues look back on the inertia of your Church, and the intrusive and decisive heroism of Damien, with something almost to be called remorse. I am sure it is so with yourself; I am persuaded your letter was inspired by a certain envy, not essentially ignoble, and the one human trait to be espied in that performance. You were thinking of the lost chance, the past day; of that which should have been conceived and was not; of the service due and not rendered. *Time was,* said the voice in your ear, in your pleasant room, as you sat raging and writing; and if the words written were base beyond parallel, the rage, I am happy to repeat—it is the only compliment I shall pay you— the rage was almost virtuous. But, sir, when we have failed, and another has succeeded; when we have stood by, and another has stepped in; when we sit and grow bulky in our charming mansions, and a plain, uncouth peasant steps into the battle, under the eyes of God, and succours the afflicted and consoles the dying, and is himself afflicted in his turn, and dies upon the field of honour—the battle cannot be retrieved as your unhappy irritation has suggested. It is a lost battle, and lost for ever. One thing remained to you in your defeat—some rags of common honour; and these you have made haste to cast away.

Common honour; not the honour of having done anything right, but the honour of not having done aught conspicuously foul; the honour of the inert: that was what remained to you. We are not all expected to be Damiens; a man may conceive his duty more narrowly, he may love his comforts better; and none will cast a stone at him for that. But will a gentleman of your reverend profession allow me an example from the fields of gallantry? When two gentlemen compete for the favour of a lady, and the one succeeds and the other is rejected, and (as will sometimes happen) matter damaging to the successful rival's credit reaches the ear of the defeated, it is held by plain men of no pretensions that his mouth is, in the circumstance, almost necessarily closed. Your Church and Damien's were in Hawaii upon a rivalry to do well: to help, to edify, to set divine examples. You having (in one huge instance) failed, and Damien succeeded, I marvel it should not have occurred to you that you were doomed to silence; that when you had been outstripped in that high rivalry, and sat inglorious in the midst of your well-being, in your pleasant room—and Damien, crowned with glories and horrors, toiled and rotted in that pigsty of his under the cliffs of Kalawao—you, the elect who would not, were the last man on earth to collect and propagate gossip on the volunteer who would and did.

I think I see you—for I try to see you in the flesh as I write these sentences—I think I see you leap at the word pigsty, a hyperbolical expression at the best. "He had no hand in the reforms," he was "a coarse, dirty man"; these were your own words; and you may think it possible that I am come to support you with fresh evidence. In a sense, it is even so. Damien has been too much depicted with a conventional halo and conventional features; so drawn by men who perhaps had not the eye to remark or the pen to express the individual; or who perhaps were only blinded and silenced by generous admiration, such as I partly envy for myself—such as you, if your soul were enlightened, would envy on your bended knees. It is the least defect of such a method of portraiture that it makes the path easy for the devil's advocate, and leaves for the misuse of the slanderer a considerable field of truth. For the truth that is suppressed by friends is the readiest weapon of the enemy. The world, in your despite, may perhaps owe you something, if your letter be the means of substituting once for all a credible likeness for a wax abstraction. For, if that world at all remember you, on the day when Damien of Molokai shall be named Saint, it will be in virtue of one work: your letter to the Reverend H. B. Gage.

You may ask on what authority I speak. It was my inclement destiny to become acquainted, not with Damien, but with Dr Hyde. When I visited the lazaretto, Damien was already in his resting grave. But such information as I have, I gathered on the spot in conversation with those who knew him well and long: some indeed who revered his memory; but others who had sparred and wrangled with him, who beheld him with no halo, who perhaps regarded him with small respect, and through whose unprepared and scarcely partial communications the plain, human features of the man shone on me convincingly. These gave me what knowledge I possess; and I learnt it in that scene where it could be most completely and sensitively understood—Kalawao, which you have never visited, about which you have never so much as endeavoured to inform yourself; for, brief as your letter is, you have found the means to stumble into that confession. "*Less than one-half* of the island," you say, "is devoted to the lepers." Molokai—"*Molokai ahina,*" the "grey," lofty, and most desolate island—along all its northern side plunges a front of precipice into a sea of unusual profundity. This range of cliff is, from east to west, the true end and the frontier of the island. Only in one spot there projects into the ocean a certain triangular and rugged down, grassy, stony, windy, and rising in the midst into a hill with a dead crater: the whole bearing to the cliff that overhangs it somewhat the same relation as a bracket to a wall. With this hint you will now be able to pick out the leper station on a map; you will be able to judge how much of Molokai is thus cut off between the surf and precipice, whether less than a half, or less than a quarter, of a fifth, or a tenth—or, say, a twentieth; and the next time you burst into print you will be in a position to share with us the issue of your calculations.

I imagine you to be one of those persons who talk with cheerfulness of that place which oxen and wain-ropes could not drag you to behold. You, who do not even know its situation on the map, probably denounce sensational descriptions, stretching your limbs the while in your pleasant parlour on Beretania Street. When I was pulled ashore there one early morning, there sat with me in the boat two sisters, bidding farewell (in humble imitation of Damien) to the lights and joys of human life. One of these wept silently; I could not withhold myself from joining her. Had you been there, it is my belief that nature would have triumphed even in you; and as the boat drew but a little nearer, and you beheld the stairs crowded with abominable deformations of our common manhood, and saw yourself landing in the midst of such a population as only now and then surrounds us in the horror of a nightmare—what a haggard eye you would have rolled over your reluctant shoulder towards the house on Beretania Street! Had you gone on; had you found every fourth face a blot upon the landscape; had you visited the hospital and seen the buttends of human beings lying there almost unrecognisable, but still breathing, still thinking, still remembering; you would have understood that life in the lazaretto is an ordeal from which the nerves of a man's spirit shrink, even as his eye quails under the brightness of the sun; you would have felt it was (even to-day) a pitiful place to visit and a hell to dwell in. It is not the fear of possible infection. That seems a little thing when compared with the pain, the pity, and the disgust of the visitor's surroundings, and the atmosphere of affliction, disease, and physical disgrace in which he breathes. I do not think I am a man more than usually timid; but I never recall the days and nights I spent upon that island promontory (eight days and seven nights), without heartfelt thankfulness that I am somewhere else. I find in my diary that I speak of my stay as a "grinding experience": I have once jotted in the margin, "*Harrowing* is the word"; and when the *Molokii* bore me at last towards the outer world, I kept repeating to myself, with a new conception of their pregnancy, those simple words of the song—

" 'Tis the most distressful country that ever yet was seen."

And observe: that which I saw and suffered from was a settlement purged, bettered, beautified; the new village built, the hospital and the Bishop-Home excellently arranged; the sisters, the doctor, and the missionaries, all indefatigable in their noble tasks. It was a different place when Damien came there and made his great renunciation, and slept that first night under a tree

21

amidst his rotting brethren: alone with pestilence; and looking forward (with what courage, with what pitiful sinkings of dread, God only knows) to a lifetime of dressing sores and stumps.

You will say, perhaps, I am too sensitive, that sights as painful abound in cancer hospitals and are confronted daily by doctors and nurses. I have long learned to admire and envy the doctors and the nurses. But there is no cancer hospital so large and populous as Kalawao and Kalaupapa; and in such a matter every fresh case, like every inch of length in the pipe of an organ, deepens the note of the impression; for what daunts the onlooker is that monstrous sum of human suffering by which he stands surrounded. Lastly, no doctor or nurse is called upon to enter once for all the doors of that gehenna; they do not say farewell, they need not abandon hope, on its sad threshold; they but go for a time to their high calling, and can look forward as they go to relief, to recreation, and to rest. But Damien shut-to with his own hand the doors of his own sepulchre.

I shall now extract three passages from my diary at Kalawao.

A. "Damien is dead and already somewhat ungratefully remembered in the field of his labours and sufferings. 'He was a good man, but very officious,' says one. Another tells me he had fallen (as other priests so easily do) into something of the ways and habits of thought of a Kanaka; but he had the wit to recognise the fact, and the good sense to laugh at" [over] "it. A plain man it seems he was; I cannot find he was a popular."

B. "After Ragsdale's death" [Ragsdale was a famous Luna, or overseer, of the unruly settlement] "there followed a brief term of office by Father Damien which served only to publish the weakness of that noble man. He was rough in his ways, and he had no control. Authority was relaxed; Damien's life was threatened, and he was soon eager to resign."

C. "Of Damien I begin to have an idea. He seems to have been a man of the peasant class, certainly of the peasant type: shrewd, ignorant and bigoted, yet with an open mind, and capable of receiving and digesting a reproof if it were bluntly administered; superbly generous in the least thing as well as in the greatest, and as ready to give his last shirt (although not without human grumbling) as he had been to sacrifice his life; essentially indiscreet and officious, which made him a troublesome colleague; domineering in all his ways, which made him incurably unpopular with the Kanakas, but yet destitute of real authority, so that his boys laughed at him and he must carry out his wishes by the means of bribes. He learned to have a mania for doctoring; and set up the Kanakas against the remedies of his regular rivals: perhaps (if anything matters at all in the treatment of such a disease) the worst thing that he did, and certainly the easiest. The best and worst of the man appear very plainly in his dealings with Mr Chapman's money; he had originally laid it out" [intended to lay it out] "entirely for the benefit of Catholics, and even so not wisely; but after a long, plain talk, he admitted his error fully and revised the list. The sad state of the boy's home is in part the result of his lack of control; in part, of his own slovenly ways and false ideas of hygiene. Brother officials used to call it 'Damien's Chinatown.' 'Well,' they would say, 'your Chinatown keeps growing.' And he would laugh with perfect good-nature, and adhere to his errors with perfect obstinacy. So much I have gathered of truth about this plain, noble human brother and father of ours; his imperfections are the traits of his face, by which we know him for our fellow; his martyrdom and his example nothing can lessen or annul; and only a person here on the spot can properly appreciate their greatness."

I have set down these private passages, as you perceive, without correction; thanks to you, the public has them in their bluntness. They are almost a list of the man's faults, for it is rather these that I was seeking:

with his virtues, with the heroic profile of his life, I and the world were already sufficiently acquainted. I was besides a little suspicious of Catholic testimony; in no ill sense, but merely because Damien's admirers and disciples were the least likely to be critical. I know you will be more suspicious still; and the facts set down above were one and all collected from the lips of Protestants who had opposed the father in his life. Yet I am strangely deceived, or they build up the image of a man, with all his weaknesses, essentially heroic, and alive with rugged honesty, generosity, and mirth.

Take it for what it is, rough private jottings of the worst sides of Damien's character, collected from the lips of those who had laboured with and (in your own phrase) "knew the man";—though I question whether Damien would *have said that he knew you.* Take it, and observe with wonder how well you were served by your gossips, how ill by your intelligence and sympathy; in how many points of fact we are at one, and how widely our appreciations vary. There is something wrong here; either with you or me. It is possible, for instance, that you, who seem to have so many ears in Kalawao, had heard of the affair of Mr Chapman's money, and were singly struck by Damien's intended wrong-doing. I was struck with that also, and set it fairly down; but I was struck much more by the fact that he had the honesty of mind to be convinced. I may here tell you that it was a long business; that one of his colleagues sat with him late into the night, multiplying arguments and accusations; that the father listened as usual with "perfect good-nature and perfect obstinacy"; but at the last, when he was persuaded—"Yes," said he, "I am very much obliged to you; you have done me a service; it would have been a theft." There are many (not Catholics merely) who require their heroes and saints to be infallible; to these the story will be painful; not to the true lovers, patrons, and servants of mankind.

And I take it, this is a type of our division; that you are one of those who have an eye for faults and failures; that you take a pleasure to find and publish them; and that, having found them, you make haste to forget the overvailing virtues and the real success which had alone introduced them to your knowledge. It is a dangerous frame of mind. That you may understand how dangerous, and into what a situation it has already brought you, we will (if you please) go hand-in-hand through the different phrases of your letter, and candidly examine each from the point of view of its truth, its appositeness, and its charity.

Damien was *coarse.*

It is very possible. You make us sorry for the lepers, who had only a coarse old peasant for their friend and father. But you, who were so refined, why were you not there, to cheer them with the lights of culture? Or may I remind you that we have some reason to doubt if John the Baptist were genteel; and in the case of Peter, on whose career you doubtless dwell approvingly in the pulpit, no doubt at all he was a "coarse, headstrong" fisherman! Yet even in our Protestant Bibles Peter is called Saint.

Damien was *dirty.*

He was. Think of the poor lepers annoyed with this dirty comrade! But the clean Dr Hyde was at his food in a fine house.

Damien was *headstrong.*

I believe you are right again; and I thank God for his strong head and heart.

Damien was *bigoted.*

I am not fond of bigots myself, because they are not fond of me. But what is meant by bigotry, that we should regard it as a blemish in a priest? Damien believed his own religion with the simplicity of a peasant or a child; as I would I could suppose that you do. For this, I wonder at him some way off; and had this been his only character, should have avoided him in life. But the point of interest in Damien, which has caused him to be so much talked about and made him at last the subject of your pen and mine, was that, in him, his bigotry, his intense and narrow faith, wrought potently for good, and strengthened him to be one of the world's heroes and exemplars.

Damien *was not sent to Molokai, but went there without orders.*

Is this a misreading? or do you really mean the words for blame? I have heard Christ, in the pulpits of our Church, held up for imitation on the ground that His sacrifice was voluntary. Does Dr Hyde think otherwise?

Damien *did not stay at the settlement, etc.*

It is true he was allowed many indulgences. Am I to understand that you blame the father for profiting by these, or the officers for granting them? In either case, it is a mighty Spartan standard to issue from the house on Beretania Street; and I am convinced you will find yourself with few supporters.

Damien *had no hand in the reforms, etc.*

I think even you will admit that I have already been frank in my description of the man I am defending; but before I take you up upon this head, I will be franker still, and tell you that perhaps nowhere in the world can a man taste a more pleasurable sense of contrast than when he passes from Damien's "Chinatown" at

Kalawao to the beautiful Bishop-Home at Kalaupapa. At this point, in my desire to make all fair for you, I will break my rule and adduce Catholic testimony. Here is a passage from my diary about my visit to the Chinatown, from which you will see how it is (even now) regarded by its own officials: "We went round all the dormitories, refectories, etc.—dark and dingy enough, with a superficial cleanliness, which he" [Mr Dutton, the lay-brother] "did not seek to defend. 'It is almost decent,' said he; 'the sisters will make that all right when we get them here.'" And yet I gathered it was already better since Damien was dead, and far better than when he was there alone and had his own (not always excellent) way. I have now come far enough to meet you on a common ground of fact; and I tell you that, to a mind not prejudiced by jealousy, all the reforms of the lazaretto, and even those which he most vigorously opposed, are properly the work of Damien. They are the evidence of his success; they are what his heroism provoked from the reluctant and the careless. Many were before him in the field; Mr Meyer, for instance, of whose faithful work we hear too little: there have been many since; and some had more worldly wisdom, though none had more devotion, than our saint. Before his day, even you will confess, they had effected little. It was his part, by one striking act of martyrdom, to direct all men's eyes on that distressful country. At a blow, and with the price of his life, he made the place illustrious and public. And that, if you will consider largely, was the one reform needful; pregnant of all that should succeed. It brought money; it brought (best individual addition of them all) the sisters; it brought supervision, for public opinion and public interest landed with the men at Kalawao. If ever a man brought reforms, and died to bring them, it was he. There is not a clean cup or towel in the Bishop-Home, but dirty Damien washed it.

Damien *was not a pure man in his relations with women, etc.*

How do you know that? Is this the nature of the conversation in that house on Beretania Street which the cabman envied, driving past?—racy details of the misconduct of the poor peasant priest, toiling under the cliffs of Molokai?

Many have visited the station before me; they seem not to have heard the rumour. When I was there I heard many shocking tales, for my informants were men speaking with the plainness of the laity; and I heard plenty of complaints of Damien. Why was this never mentioned? and how came it to you in the retirement of your clerical parlour?

But I must not even seem to deceive you. This scandal, when I read it in your letter, was not new to me. I had heard it once before; and I must tell you how.

There came to Samoa a man from Honolulu; he, in a public-house on the beach, volunteered the statement that Damien had "contracted the disease from having connection with the female lepers"; and I find a joy in telling you how the report was welcomed in a public-house. A man sprang to his feet; I am not at liberty to give his name, but from what I heard I doubt if you would care to have him to dinner in Beretania Street. "You miserable little—" (here is a word I dare not print, it would so shock your ears). "You miserable little—," he cried, "if the story were a thousand times true, can't you see you are a million times a lower—for daring to repeat it?" I wish it could be told of you that when the report reached you in your house, perhaps after family worship, you had found in your soul enough holy anger to receive it with the same expressions; ay, even with that one which I dare not print; it would not need to have been blotted away, like Uncle Toby's oath, by the tears of the recording angel ["The accusing spirit which flew up to heaven's chancery with the oath blushed as he gave it in; and the recording angel, as he wrote it down, dropped a tear upon the word and blotted it out for ever."—*Lawrence Sterne*]; it would have been counted to you for your brightest righteousness. But you have deliberately chosen the part of the man from Honolulu, and you have played it with improvements of your own. The man from Honolulu—miserable, leering creature—communicated the tale to a rude knot of beachcombing drinkers in a public-house, where (I will so far agree with your temperance opinions) man is not always at his noblest; and the man from Honolulu had himself been drinking—drinking, we may charitably fancy, to excess. It was to your "Dear Brother, the Reverend H. B. Gage," that you chose to communicate the sickening story; and the blue ribbon which adorns your portly bosom forbids me to allow you the extenuating plea that you were drunk when it was done. Your "dear brother"—a brother indeed—made haste to deliver up your letter (as a means of grace, perhaps) to the religious papers; where, after many months, I found and read and wondered at it; and whence I have now reproduced it for the wonder of others. And you and your dear brother have, by this cycle of operations, built up a contrast very edifying to examine in detail. The man whom you would not care to have to dinner, on the one side; on the other, the Reverend Dr Hyde and the Reverend H. B. Gage: the Apia barroom, the Honolulu manse.

But I fear you scarce appreciate how you appear to your fellow-men; and to bring it home to you, I will suppose your story to be true. I will suppose—and God forgive me for supposing it—that Damien faltered and stumbled in his narrow path of duty; I will suppose that, in the horror of his isolation, perhaps in the fever of incipient disease, he, who was doing so much more than he had sworn, failed in the letter of his priestly oath—he, who was so much a better man that either you or me, who did what we have never dreamed of daring—he too tasted of our common frailty. "O Iago, the pity of it!" The least tender should be moved to tears; the most incredulous to prayer. And all that you could do was to pen your letter to the Reverend H.B. Gage!

Is it growing at all clear to you what a picture you have drawn of your own heart? I will try yet once again to make it clearer. You had a father: suppose this tale were about him, and some informant brought it to you, proof in hand: I am not making too high an estimate of your emotional nature when I suppose you would regret the circumstance? that you would feel the tale of frailty the more keenly since it shamed the author of your days? and that the last thing you would do would be to publish it in the religious press? Well, the man who tried to do what Damien did, is my father, and the father of the man in the Apia bar, and the father of all who love goodness; and he was your father too, if God had given you grace to see it.

WHERE ALL ROADS LEAD

G K Chesterton

I
THE YOUTH OF THE CHURCH

Until about the end of the nineteenth century a
man was expected to give his reasons for joining the
Catholic Church. Today a man is really expected to
give his reasons for not joining it. This may seem an
exaggeration; but I believe it to stand for a subconscious
truth in thousands of minds. As for the fundamental
reasons for a man doing it, there are only two that are
really fundamental. One is that he believes it to be the
solid objective truth, which is true whether he likes it or
not; and the other that he seeks liberation from his sins.
If there be any man for whom these are not the main
motives it is idle to enquire what were his philosophical
or historical or emotional reasons for joining the old
religion; for he has not joined it at all.

THE CHALLENGE OF THE CHURCH

But a preliminary word or two may well be said about
the other matter, which may be called the challenge
of the Church. I mean that the world has recently
become aware of that challenge in a curious and

almost creepy fashion. I am literally one of the least, because one of the latest, of a crowd of converts who have been thinking along the same lines as I. There has been a happy increase in the number of Catholics; but there has also been, if I may so express it, a happy increase in the number of non-Catholics; in the sense of conscious non-Catholics. The world has become conscious that it is not Catholic. Only lately it would have been about as likely to brood on the fact that it was not Confucian; and all the array of reasons for not joining the Church of Rome marked but the beginning of the ultimate reason for joining it. At this stage, let it be understood, I am speaking of a reaction and rejection which was, as mine would once have been, honestly if conventionally convinced. I am not speaking now of the stage of mere self-deception or sulky excuses; though such a stage there may be before the end. I am remarking that even while we truly think that the reasons are reasonable, we tacitly assume that the reasons are required. Far back at the beginning of all our changes, if I may speak for many much better than myself, there was the idea that we must have reasons for joining the Catholic Church. I never had any reasons for not joining the Greek Church, or the religion of Mahomet, or the Theosophical Society, or the Society of Friends. Doubtless, I could have discovered and defined the reasons had they been demanded, just as

I could have found the reasons for not going to live in Lithuania, or not being a chartered accountant, or not changing my name to Vortigern Brown, or not doing a thousand other things that it had never occurred to me to do. But the point is that I never felt the presence or pressure of a possibility at all. I heard no distant and distracting voice calling me to Lithuania or to Islam; I had no itch to explain to myself why my name was not Vortigern or why my religion was not Theosophy. That sort of presence and pressure of the Church I believe to be universal and ubiquitous today; not only among Anglicans, but among Agnostics. I repeat that I do not mean that they have no real objections; on the contrary, I mean that they have begun really to object; they have begun to kick and struggle.

A YOUNG RELIGION

Now I have noted first this common consciousness of the challenge of the Church, because I believe it to be connected with something else. That something else is the strongest of all the purely intellectual forces that dragged me towards the truth. It is not merely the survival of the faith, but the singular nature of its survival. I have called it by a conventional phrase, the old religion. But it is not an old religion; it is a religion that refuses to grow old. At the moment of history it is a very young religion; rather especially a religion of young men. It is much newer than the new religions; its young men are more fiery, more full of their subject, more eager to explain and argue, than were the young Socialists of my own youth. It does not merely stand firm like an old guard; it has recaptured the initiative and is conducting the counter-attack. In short, it is what youth always is, rightly or wrongly; it is aggressive. It is this atmosphere of the aggressiveness of Catholicism that has thrown the old intellectuals on the defensive. It is this that has produced the almost morbid self-consciousness of which I have spoken. The converts are truly fighting, in those words which recur like a burden at the opening of the Mass, for a thing which giveth joy to their youth. I cannot understand how this unearthly freshness in something so old can possibly be explained except on a supposition that it is indeed unearthly.

It is not true, as the rationalist histories imply, that through the ages orthodoxy has grown old slowly. It is rather heresy that has grown old quickly. The Reformation grew old amazingly quickly. It was the Counter-Reformation that grew young. In England, it is strange to note how soon Puritanism turned into Paganism, or perhaps ultimately into Philistinism. It is strange to note how soon the Puritans degenerated into Whigs. By the end of the seventeenth century

English politics had dried up into a wrinkled cynicism that might have been as old as Chinese etiquette. It was the Counter-Reformation that was full of the fire and even of the impatience of youth. It was in the Catholic figures of the sixteenth and seventeenth centuries that we find the spirit of energy, in the only noble sense of novelty. It was people like St Teresa who reformed; people like Bossuet who challenged; people like Pascal who questioned; people like Suarez who speculated. The counter-attack was like a charge of the old spears of chivalry. And indeed the comparison is very relevant to the generalization. I believe that this renovation, which has certainly happened in our own time, and which has certainly happened in a time so recent as the Reformation, has really happened again and again in the history of Christendom.

A FLAMING TORCH

Working backwards on the same principle, I will mention at least two examples which I suspect to have been similar; the case of Islam and the case of Arianism. The Church had any number of opportunities of dying, and even of being respectfully interred. But the younger generation always began once again to knock at the door; and never louder than when it was knocking at the lid of the coffin in which it had been prematurely buried. Islam and Arianism were both attempts to broaden the basis to a sane and simple Theism, the former supported by great military success and the latter by great imperial prestige. They ought to have finally established the new system, but for the one perplexing fact, that the old system preserved the only seed and secret of novelty. Anyone reading between the lines of the twelfth-century record can see that the world was permeated by potential Pantheism and Paganism; we can see it in the dread of the Arabian version of Aristotle, in the rumour about great men being Moslems in secret; the old men, seeing the simple faith of the Dark Ages dissolving, might well have thought that the fading of Christendom into Islam would be the next thing to happen. If so, the old men would have been much surprised at what did happen. What did happen was a roar like thunder from thousands and thousands of young men, throwing all their youth into one exultant counter-charge: the Crusades. The actual effect of danger from the younger religion was renewal of our own youth. It was the sons of St Francis, the Jugglers of God, wandering singing over all the roads of the world; it was the Gothic going up like a flight of arrows; it was a rejuvenation of Europe. And though I know less of the older period, I suspect that the same was true of Athanasian orthodoxy in revolt against

Arian officialism. The older men had submitted it to a compromise, and St Athanasius led the younger like a divine demagogue. The persecuted carried into exile the sacred fire. It was a flaming torch that could be cast out, but could not be trampled out.

CATHOLICISM ON THE MARCH

Whenever Catholicism is driven out as an old thing, it always returns as a new thing...It is not a survival. This then is the vital distinction, upon which I have dwelt before going further, because its comprehension concerns the argument later on. It is not endurance, but the *kind* of recovery. Doubtless there are, in every such transition, groups of good and even glorious Catholics who have held their religion rather as a thing of the past; and I have far too much admiration for their religious loyalty to insist here on any regrets for their reactionary politics. It is possible to look back to the passing of the monks merely as one looks back to the passing of the Stuarts; it is possible to look back to the passing of the Stuarts merely as one looks back to the passing of the Druids. But Catholicism is not the thing that faded with the final failure of the Jacobites; rather it is a thing that returned with a rush after the relative failure of the Jacobins. There may have been an ecclesiastic surviving from the Dark Ages who did not understand the new movement of the Middle Ages; there certainly were good Catholics who did not see the need for the great raid of the Jesuits or the reforms of St Teresa; and they were most probably much better people than we are. But rejuvenation does recur; and it is the first fact with which I wish to start my argument…For the moment I am content to say that we live in one of those recurrent periods of Catholicism on the march; and to draw a more simple moral from it. The real honour is due to those who were with it when its cause seemed hopeless; and no credit, beyond that of common intelligence, really belongs to anyone who has joined it when it is so evidently the hope of the world.

II
THE CASE FOR COMPLEXITY

I began with the power of the Church to grow young suddenly, when she is expected to grow old slowly, and remarked that this power in a creed was one which I could only conceive as thus regularly recurrent under two conditions: first, that it was really true; and second, that the power in it was more than mortal. In the ultimate sense, these are undoubtedly the reasons for what is a revolution that really returns like the revolution of a wheel. But among the secondary and superficial causes of this rejuvenation may be specially noted, I fancy, the very fact of which religious reformers have so constantly complained; I mean the complexity of the creeds. There is a sense in which the Faith is the simplest of religions; but there is another sense in which it really is by far the most complicated. And what I emphasize here is that, contrary to many modern notions, it owes its victory over modern minds to its complexity and not its simplicity. It owes its most recent revivals to the very fact that it is the one creed that is still not ashamed of being complicated…

We have had during the last few centuries a series of extremely simple religions; each indeed trying to be more simple than the last. And the manifest mark of all these simplifications was, not only that they were finally sterile, but that they were rapidly stale. A man had said the last word about them when he had said the first. Atheism is, I suppose, the supreme example of a simple faith. The man says there is no God; if he really says it in his heart, he is a certain sort of man so designated in Scripture. But anyhow, when he has said it, he has said it; and there seems to be no more to be said. The conversation seems likely to languish. The truth is that the atmosphere of excitement by which the atheist lived was an atmosphere of thrilled and shuddering theism, and not of atheism at all; it was an atmosphere of defiance and not of denial. Irreverence is a very servile parasite of reverence, and has starved with its starving lord. After this first fuss about the merely aesthetic effect of blasphemy, the whole thing vanishes into its own void. If there were no God, there would be no atheists.

It is easy to say this of the nineteenth century negation, for that sort of atheism is already one of the dead heresies. But what is not always noticed is that all the modern forms of theism have the same blank. Theism is as negative as atheism. To say with the optimists that God is good and therefore everything is good, or with the universalists that God is love and therefore everything is love, or with the Christian Scientists that God is spirit and therefore everything is spirit, or for that matter with the pessimists that God is cruel and therefore everything is a beastly shame; to say any of these things is to make a remark to which it is difficult to make any reply, except 'Oh', or possibly, in a rather feeble fashion, 'Well, well'. The statement is certainly in one sense very complete; possibly a little too complete, and we find ourselves wishing it were a little more complex. And that is exactly the point. It is not complex enough to be a living organism. It has no vitality because it has no variety of function.

One broad characteristic belongs to all the schools of thought that are called broad-minded, and that is that their eloquence ends in a sort of silence not very far removed from sleep. One mark distinguishes all the wild innovations and insurrections of modern intellectualism; one note is apparent in all the new and revolutionary religions that have recently swept the world; and that note is dullness. They are too simple to be true. And meanwhile any one Catholic peasant, while holding one small bead of the rosary in his fingers, can be conscious, not of one eternity, but of a complex and almost a conflict of eternities; as, for example, in the relations of Our Lord and Our Lady, of the fatherhood and childhood of God, of the motherhood and childhood of Mary. Thoughts of that kind have in a supernatural sense something analogous to sex; they breed. They are fruitful and multiply; and there is no end to them. They have innumerable aspects; but the aspect that concerns the argument here is this: that a religion which is rich in this sense always has a number of ideas in reserve. Besides the ideas that are being applied to a particular problem of a particular period, there are a number of rich fields of thought which are in that sense lying fallow. Where a new theory, invented to meet a new problem, rapidly perishes with that problem, the old things are always waiting for other problems when they shall in their turn become new. A new Catholic movement is generally a movement to emphasize some Catholic idea that was only neglected in the sense that it was not till then specially needed; but when it was needed, nothing else can meet the need. In other words, the only way really to meet all the human needs of the future is to pass into the possession of all the Catholic thoughts of the past; and the only way to do that is really to become a Catholic.

THE RESERVES OF THE PAST

In these notes I do not intend to say anything in very direct criticism of the Anglican Church or the Anglo-Catholic theory, because I know it in my own case to be the worst possible way to go to work. The Church drew me out of Anglicanism as the very idea of Our Lady drew me along before out of ordinary Protestantism by being herself, that is, by being beautiful. I was converted by the positive attractions of the things I had not yet got, and not by negative disparagements of such things as I had managed to get already. When these disparagements were uttered they generally had, almost against my will, the opposite effect to that intended; the effect of a slight setback.

I think in my heart I was already hoping that Roman Catholics would really prove to have more charity and humility than anybody else, and anything that even seemed to savour of the opposite was judged by too sensitive a standard in the mood of that moment. I am, therefore, very anxious not to make that sort of mistake myself. It would be easy to put, in a much shorter and sharper fashion, the conclusion to which I and every other convert have eventually come. It would be easy to argue merely that our whole position was a common contradiction; since we were always arguing that England had suffered in a thousand ways from being Protestant, and yet at the same time arguing that she had remained Catholic. It would be easy, and in a sense only too true, to call the whole thing a piece of English half-conscious hypocrisy; an attempt to remedy a mistake without admitting it. Nor do I deny that there are High-Churchmen who provoke and perhaps deserve this tone, by talking as if Catholicism had never been betrayed and oppressed. To them indeed one is tempted to say that St Peter denied his Lord; but at least he never denied that he had denied Him.

But of most souls in such a transition the truth is far more subtle; and of all I knew far more sympathetic; and I have deliberately approached this problem by a route that may seem circuitous, but which I believe to be the right approach in such a problem of subtlety and sympathy. The first fact to be pointed out, I think, to the honest and doubtful Anglican is that this power of resurrection in the Church does depend on this possession of reserves in the Church. To have this power, it is necessary to possess the whole past of the religion, and not merely those parts of it that seemed obviously needed in the nineteenth century by the men of the Oxford Movement, or in the twentieth century by the men of the Anglo-Catholic Congress. They did discover the need of Catholic things, and they did discover the need of one thing at a time. They took their pick in the fields of Christendom, but they did not possess the fields; and above all, they did not possess the fallow fields. They could not have all the riches, because they could not have all the reserves of the religion.

We have a great many predictions of the future, which are only rather dull extensions of the present. Very few moderns have dared to imagine the future as anything but modern. Most of them have gone mad with the attempt to imagine their great-grandchildren as exactly like themselves, only more so. But the Church is Futurist in the only sane sense, just as she is individualist in the only sane sense, or Socialist in the only sane sense. That is, she is prepared for problems which are utterly different from the problems of today. Now I think the truth about a man who calls himself, as I did, an Anglo-Catholic, may most fairly and sympathetically be stated thus. He is, of course, in strict definition a heretic, but he is not a heresiarch. He is not founding a heresy of the moment; but he is merely *fighting* a heresy at the moment. Even when he is defending orthodoxy, as he so often is, he is only defending it upon certain points against certain fallacies. But the fallacies are only fashions, and the next fashion will be quite different. And then *his* orthodoxy will be old-fashioned, but not ours.

III
THE STORY OF A HALF-TRUTH

By this time it must be obvious that every single thing in the Catholic Church which was condemned by the modern world has been reintroduced by the modern world, and always in a lower form. The Puritans rejected art and symbolism, and the Decadents brought them back again with all the old appeal to sense and an additional appeal to sensuality. The rationalists rejected supernatural healing and it was brought back by Yankee charlatans who not only proclaimed supernatural healing, but forbade natural healing. Protestant moralists abolished the confessional and the

Psychoanalysts have re-established the confessional, with every one of its alleged dangers and not one of its admitted safeguards. The Protestant patriots resented the intervention of an international faith, and went on to evolve an empire entangled in international finance. Having complained that the family was insulted by monasticism, they have lived to see the family broken in pieces by bureaucracy; having objected to fasts being appointed for anybody during any exceptional interval, they have survived to see teetotallers and vegetarians trying to impose a fast on everybody for ever.

All this, as I say, has become obvious, but there is a further development of the truth with which I am more especially dealing here; which concerns not so much the case of these general movements which may almost be called vulgar errors, but rather the case of certain individual ideas that are private inspirations of the individual. A young man may, without any very offensive vanity, come to the conclusion that he has something to say. He may think that a truth is missed in the current controversies and that he himself may remind the world of it in a tolerably lucid or pointed fashion. It seems to me that there are two courses that he can follow; and I wish to suggest them here because there must be a good many young men in that position, because I have been in it myself and because I may be said in some sense to have followed both courses, first one and then the other. He can take his truth, or half-truth, into the bustle and confusion of the modern world, of general secular society, and pit it against all the other notions that are being urged in this way… In that case it is likely enough that he will be hailed by journalists as having a 'message'; it is, at any rate, probable that he will have a vogue; but it is not very clear that anything will happen to his idea in the long run…and even though he may have done as well as he could reasonably expect for himself, it is not clear that he has done very much for the world; especially when the world is in a mood that permits nothing but fashions and forgetfulness. But there is a much greater danger in his position. Even supposing that his truth does become a tradition, it will only harden into a heresy. For it can only harden as the half-truth that it is; and even if it was true in its lifetime, it will have become false when it is fossilized. Sometimes a few touches from fanatical followers can turn it into a most extravagant and horrible falsehood…The moral is that the half-truth must be linked up with the whole truth – and who is to link it up? Herod the tyrant must not massacre babies because they would have been glad of a few months of life when they were babes unborn. A man must not be a slave on the plea that even a slave can see a dandelion. A man must not be thrown into gaol in defiance of justice because he will still see a patch of daylight on the wall. In a word, wonder and humility and gratitude are good things, but they are not the only good things; and there must be something to make the poet who praises them admit that justice and mercy and human dignity are good things too. Knowing something of the nature of a modern poet captured by a modern fancy, I can only see one thing in the world that is in the least likely to do it.

I have said that there are two courses for the young man specializing in the half-truth. I have given a personal example of him and the possibility of his horrible end. The other course is that he should take his half-truth into the culture of the Catholic Church, which really is a culture and where it really will be cultivated. For that place is a garden; and the noisy world outside nowadays is none the less a wilderness because it is a howling wilderness. That is, he can take his idea where it will be valued for what is true in it, where it will be balanced by other truths and often supported by better arguments. In other words, it will become a part, however small a part, of a permanent civilization which uses its moral riches as science uses the store of facts. Thus, in the idle instance I have given, there is nothing true in that old childish mood of mine which the Catholic Church in any way condemns. She does not condemn a love of poetry or fantasy; she does not condemn, but rather commands, a sentiment of gratitude for the breath of life. Indeed, it is a spirit in which many Catholic poets have rather specialized, and its first and finest appearance, perhaps, is in the great Canticle of St Francis. But in that same spiritual society, I know that optimism will never be turned into an orgy of anarchy or a stagnation of slavery and that there will not fall on any one of us the ironical disaster of having discovered a truth only to disseminate a lie.

BACKGROUND

Fr Damien de Veuster – or, as he is now known, St Damien of Molokai – is one of the better-known examples of practical Christianity. His heroic life amongst the lepers of Molokai, and his eventual death amongst them, from leprosy, hardly, or so one would think, admits of criticism from even the professionally unreligious. Yet, for some reason, a Presbyterian minister decided to dismiss his work as useless and attack his moral character. Robert Louis Stevenson had visited Hawaii and was fascinated by Damien's life and work. His open letter answers these allegations in forcible terms.

G K Chesterton's text *Where All Roads Lead* is a fine example of his characteristic paradoxical style, which tends to make some of his readers into devotees but bring out others in the literary equivalent of a rash. His arguments draw heavily from those of his friend Hilaire Belloc, but cast them into a form at once more epigrammatic and more diffuse.

CTS ONEFIFTIES